TORONTO
MAPLE LEAFS

By Ellen Labrecque

THE CHILD'S WORLD®

1980 Lookout Drive • Mankato, MN 56003-1705
800-599-READ • www.childsworld.com

ACKNOWLEDGMENTS

The Child's World®. Mary Berendes, Publishing Director
Shoreline Publishing Group, LLC: James Buckley, Jr.,
 Production Director
The Design Lab: Gregory Lindholm, Design and
 Page Production

PHOTOS

Cover: Getty Images
Interior: AP/Wide World: 10, 13, 18, 25 top right, 25
 bottom, 27; Getty Images: 5, 6, 9, 17, 21, 22, 25 left.

LIBRARY OF CONGRESS
CATALOGING-IN-PUBLICATION DATA

Labrecque, Ellen.
  Toronto Maple Leafs / by Ellen Labrecque.
     p. cm.
  Includes bibliographical references and index.
  ISBN 978-1-60253-444-5 (library bound : alk. paper)
  1. Toronto Maple Leafs (Hockey team)—History—Juvenile
literature. I. Title.

GV848.T6L33 2010
796.962'6409713541—dc22

2010015300

Printed in the United States of America
Mankato, Minnesota
July 2010
F11538

TABLE OF CONTENTS

4   Go, Maple Leafs!

7   Who Are the Toronto Maple Leafs?

8   Where They Came From

11   Who They Play

12   Where They Play

15   The Hockey Rink

16   Big Days!

19   Tough Days!

20   Meet the Fans

23   Heroes Then...

24   Heroes Now...

26   Gearing Up

28   Sports Stats

30   Glossary

31   Find Out More

32   Index and About the Author

GO, MAPLE LEAFS!

Don't mess with the Maple Leafs! A player from the other team skates down the ice. The Maple Leafs' **goalie** is ready to stop the **puck**! Smack! The puck bounces off his pad. The goalie clears it away. Great save! Let's meet the Toronto Maple Leafs!

4

Save! This great overhead view shows another save by the Maple Leafs' goalie, Jonas Gustavsson.

Luke Schenn is one of a number of talented young Maple Leafs.

WHO ARE THE TORONTO MAPLE LEAFS?

The Toronto Maple Leafs play in the National Hockey League (NHL). They are one of 30 teams in the NHL. The NHL includes the Eastern Conference and the Western Conference. The Maple Leafs play in the Northeast Division of the Eastern Conference. The playoffs end with the winners of the Eastern and Western conferences facing off. The champion wins the **Stanley Cup**. The Maple Leafs have won 11 Stanley Cups.

WHERE THEY CAME FROM

The Maple Leafs were formed in 1917. They were one of the Original Six—the first six teams in the NHL. The Leafs won their first Stanley Cup in 1932 and won 10 more in the 1940s, 1950s and 1960s. But they haven't won any more in the last 43 years. Two-way **center** Dave Keon helped the Maple Leafs to their four Stanley Cup titles in the 1960s, including their last one in 1967.

Toronto goalie Terry Sawchuk is ready to make a save during this 1967 Stanley Cup Finals game.

Canada's top two teams—
Toronto and Montreal—always
play hard-hitting games!

WHO THEY PLAY

The Maple Leafs play 82 games each season. They play all the other teams in their division six times. The other Northeast Division teams are the Ottawa Senators, the Buffalo Sabres, the Boston Bruins, and the Montreal Canadiens. The Maple Leafs and the Canadiens are bitter **rivals**. They have faced-off in the Stanley Cup finals five times. The Maple Leafs also play other teams in the Eastern and Western Conferences.

11

WHERE THEY PLAY

The Maple Leafs play their home games in the Air Canada Centre, which was built in 1999. The **arena** is also home to the NBA's Toronto Raptors. Before 1999, the hockey team played in Maple Leaf Gardens. It was one of the most famous NHL arenas. It was also where the Maple Leafs won their 11 Stanley Cups. Maple Leaf Gardens still stands today, but it is rarely used.

Air Canada Centre gave Toronto fans a brand-new place to watch their favorite team.

13

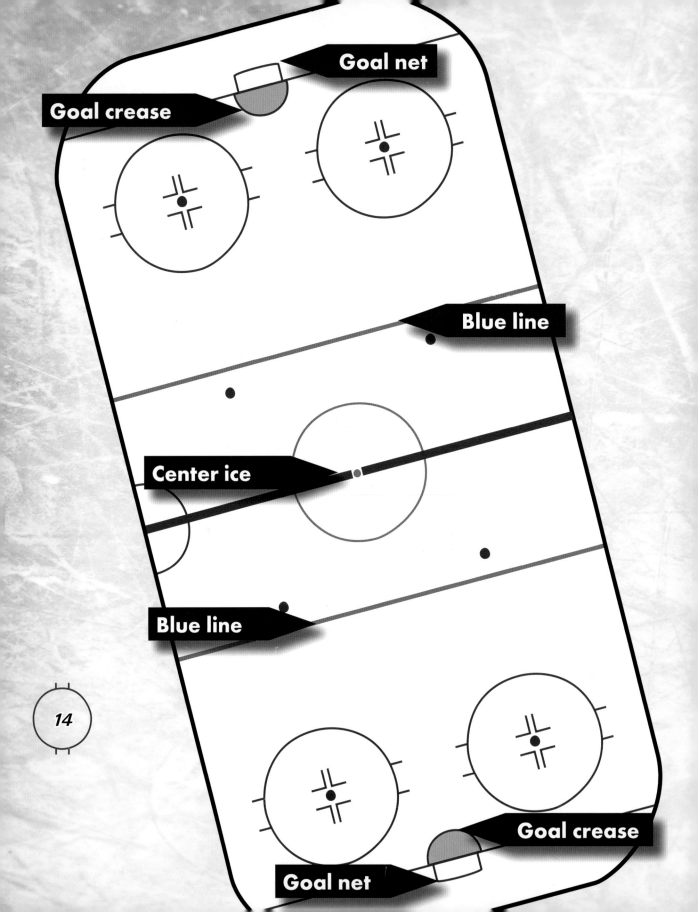

Goal net

Goal crease

Blue line

Center ice

Blue line

14

Goal crease

Goal net

THE HOCKEY RINK

Hockey games are played on a sheet of ice called a rink. It is a rounded rectangle. NHL rinks are 200 feet (61 m) long and 85 feet (26 m) wide. Wooden boards surround the entire rink. Clear plastic panels are on top of the boards so fans can see the action and be protected from flying pucks. Netting is hung above the seats at each end of the rink to catch any wild pucks. The goal nets are near each end of the rink. Each net is four feet (1.2 m) high and six feet (1.8 m) wide. A red line marks the center of the ice. Blue lines mark each team's defensive zone.

THE PUCK

An NHL puck is made of very hard rubber. The disk is three inches (76 mm) wide and 1 inch (25 mm) thick. It weighs about 6 ounces (170 g). It's black so it's easy to see on the ice. Many pucks are used during a game, because some fly into the stands.

BIG DAYS!

The Maple Leafs have had many great seasons in their long history. Here are three of the greatest:

1941–42: The Maple Leafs were behind by three games in the Stanley Cup Finals, but came back to beat the Detroit Red Wings for the championship. No team has repeated this feat since.

1966–67: The Leafs beat their rival, the Canadiens, in six games for the Stanley Cup. They won the final game, 3–1, on their home ice.

2003–04: The Leafs tied their team record for most wins in a season (45). This was also the sixth straight season Toronto made the playoffs.

During the 2004 playoffs, Darcy Tucker gets praise from his team after scoring a key goal.

Crash! That's what happened to the Maple Leafs during a disappointing 2008-09 season.

TOUGH DAYS!

Not every Maple Leaf season ends with a Stanley Cup championship. Here are some of the toughest seasons in Toronto's history.

1918–19: In just their second season in the league, Toronto finished with a terrible 5–13–0 record. It was the fewest wins the team would ever have in a season.

1984–85 The Maple Leafs finished last in their division and set a team record with 52 losses.

2008–09: Toronto missed the playoffs for the fourth straight season. The team ended up last in the division for the second season in a row.

MEET THE FANS

The Maple Leafs are very popular in hockey-crazed Canada. Fans flock to the rink to support the Leafs. The team's television ratings are usually the highest in the NHL. The Blue-and-White faithful stick with their team, despite suffering through a long championship **drought**. Leaf Nation will always remain true!

21

These fans really got into showing their love of the Leafs!

Mats Sundin went from Sweden to Canada to become an NHL star.

HEROES THEN...

The Maple Leafs have plenty of legendary stars. Here are just a few: Charlie Conacher was a powerful forward. The blazing shots of the "Big Bomber" were feared by goalies everywhere. He led the Leafs to the Cup title in 1932. Center Dave Keon was the Leafs' star during the glory years of the 1960s. Standing just 5'9", he had one of the best backhanded shots in the game. Center Mats Sundin was **captain** of the Maple Leafs for 11 seasons from 1994–2008. "Captain Clutch" still leads the Leafs in goals (420) and **points** (987).

HEROES NOW...

Leafs players are tough and skilled. Goalie Jonas Gustavsson is nicknamed "The Monster" for his size (6'3") and **clutch play**. Right **wing** Colton Orr is a tough player who is feared throughout the league because he always protects his teammates. **Defenseman** Tomas Kaberle stops shots *and* scores goals! Bruising right-winger Phil Kessel led the team in scoring in 2009–10, with 55 points. Defensman Dion Phaneuf's hard checks are some of the most feared in the NHL.

DEFENSEMAN

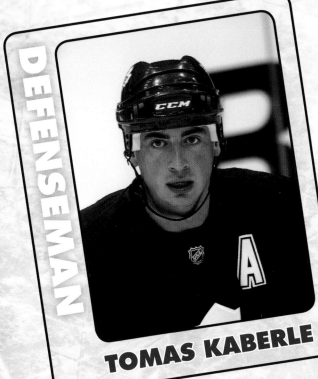

TOMAS KABERLE

RIGHT WING

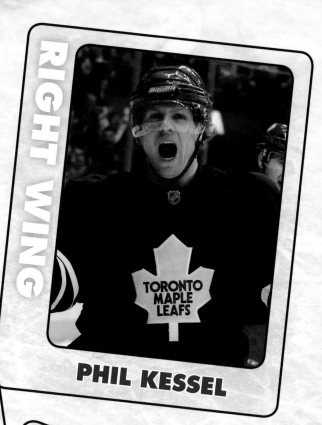

PHIL KESSEL

DEFENSEMAN

DION PHANEUF

GEARING UP

Hockey players wear short pants and a jersey called a "sweater." Underneath, they wear lots of pads to protect themselves. They also wear padded gloves and a hard plastic helmet. They wear special ice hockey skates with razor-sharp blades. They carry a stick to handle the puck.

Goalies wear special gloves to help them block and catch shots. They have extra padding on their legs, chest, and arms. They also wear special decorated helmets and use a larger stick.

26

Customized helmet

Blocker

Catching glove

Goalie stick

Leg pads

Skates with blocking blades

Helmet

Face shield

Shoulder pads

Sweater

Gloves

Knee pads

Shin guards

Skates

Stick

SPORTS STATS

Here are some all-time career records for the Toronto Maple Leafs. All the stats are through the 2009–2010 season.

GOALS

HOT SHOTS

These players have scored the most career goals for the Maple Leafs.

PLAYER	GOALS
Mats Sundin	420
Darryl Sittler	389

ASSISTS

PERFECT PASSERS

These players have the most career **assists** on the team.

PLAYER	ASSISTS
Borje Salming	620
Mats Sundin	567

POINTS

BIG SCORES!

These players have the most points, a combination of goals and assists.

PLAYER	POINTS
Mats Sundin	987
Darryl Sittler	916

SUPER SAVERS

These Toronto goalies have allowed the fewest goals per game in their career.

GOALS AGAINST AVERAGE

PLAYER	GAA
Harry Lumley	2.20
Curtis Joseph	2.49

PLAYER POSITIVE

These players have the best **plus-minus** in Maple Leafs history.

CAREER PLUS-MINUS

PLAYER	PLUS-MINUS
Borje Salming	+155
Mats Sundin	+99

FROM THE BENCH

These coaches have the most wins in Maples Leafs history.

COACHES

COACH	WINS
Punch Imlach	370
Pat Quinn	300

GLOSSARY

arena an indoor place for sports

assist a play that gives the puck to the player who scores a goal

captain a player chosen to lead his team on and off the ice

center a hockey position at the middle of the forward, offensive line

clutch play the ability of a player to come through when his team needs him most

defenseman a player who takes a position closest to his own goal, to keep the puck out

drought a long period without water, but here a long time without a title

goalie the goaltender, whose job is to keep pucks out of the net

plus-minus a player gets a plus one for being on the ice when their team scores a goal, and a minus one when the other team scores a goal; the total of these pluses and minuses creates this stat. The better players always have high plus ratings

points a team gets two points for every game they win and one point for every game they tie; a player gets a point for every goal he scores and another point for every assist

puck the hard, frozen rubber disk used when playing hockey

rivals teams that play each other often and with great intensity

Stanley Cup the trophy awarded each year to the winner of the National Hockey League championship

wing a hockey position on the outside left or right of the forward line

FIND OUT MORE

BOOKS

McAuliffe, Bill. *Toronto Maple Leafs: NHL History & Heroes*. Toronto: Saunders Book Co., 2009.

Morrison, Scott. *Mats Sundin*. Toronto: Key Porter Books, 2000.

Thomas, Kelly, and John Kicksee. *Inside Hockey!: The Legends, Facts, and Feats that Made the Game*. Toronto: Maple Leaf Press, 2008.

WEB SITES

Visit our Web page for links about the Toronto Maple Leafs and other pro hockey teams.

childsworld.com/links

Note to Parents, Teachers, and Librarians: We routinely verify our Web links to make sure they are safe, active sites—so encourage your readers to check them out!

INDEX

Air Canada Centre, 12, 13

Atlantic Division, 7, 8, 11, 19

Boston Bruins, 11
Buffalo Sabres, 11

Conacher, Charlie "The Big Bomber," 23

Detroit Red Wings, 16

Eastern Conference, 7, 11

gear, hockey, 26-27
Gustavsson, Jonas, 5, 24

Hockey Hall of Fame, 8

Imlach, Punch,

Kaberle, Tomas, 24, 25
Keon, Dave, 8, 23
Kessel, Phil, 24, 25

Maple Leaf Garden, 12
Montreal Canadiens, 10, 11, 16

Original Six, 8
Orr, Colton, 24
Ottawa Senators, 11

Phaneuf, Dion, 24, 25

Quinn, Pat, 29

Roach, John Ross, 29
Rollins, Al, 29

Salming, Borje, 28, 29
Sawchuck, Terry, 9
Schenn, Luke, 6
Sittler, Daryl, 28
Stanley Cup, 7, 8, 9, 12, 19
Sundin, Mats, 22, 23, 28, 29

Toronto Raptors, 12
Tucker, Darcy, 17

uniforms, 26-27

Western Conference, 7, 11

ABOUT THE AUTHOR

Ellen Labrecque has written dozens of books on sports for young readers. She is a big hockey fan, but admits she loves Olympic hockey as much as the NHL games!